THE POWER OF PERCEPTION WORKBOOK

DR. TAIA WILLIS, LMFT

A JOURNEY OF SELF-DISCOVERY AND TRANSFORMATION

CHRISTIAN LIVING BOOKS

ChristianLivingBooks.com
We bring your dreams to fruition.
Largo, MD

I0080646

ISBN 9781562296452

CONTENTS

INTRODUCTION

This workbook is designed to be a companion guide on your journey of self-discovery, spiritual growth, and personal transformation. Each chapter explores a different facet of perception and its impact on your life, offering insights, reflections, and practical exercises to help you deepen your understanding and apply the principles to your own experience.

1. Start with an open heart and mind: Approach each chapter with a posture of openness, curiosity, and willingness to learn. Be prepared to explore new ideas, confront uncomfortable truths, and embrace the process of growth and change.

2. Get a journal: We've provided space for key fields but be sure to keep your dedicated journal nearby. It's where you can freely capture your thoughts, revelations, and growth desires without limits. This way, you have all the room you need to truly engage in your journey.

3. Engage with the reflections and exercises: Each chapter includes a variety of reflective questions, prompts, and unique exercises tailored to the chapter's theme. They are all designed to help you personalize the insights and apply them to your life. Take time to ponder the questions, journal your responses, and complete the exercises with honesty and vulnerability.

4. Embrace the Mirror Moments: Throughout the workbook, you'll find "Mirror Moment" prompts that invite you to take a deeper look at yourself and your story. Use these opportunities to practice self-reflection, self-compassion, and self-awareness and to gain a clearer vision of who you are and who God is calling you to be.

5. Explore Transformative Insights: This section invites you to reflect on the key learnings and "aha" moments from the material. Use these prompts to identify and articulate the insights that have the potential to create significant shifts in your personal development and self-understanding and consider how you can apply them to your life for lasting growth and change.

6. Put your insights into action: The "Perception in Action" prompts offer practical ways to apply the principles and insights from each chapter to your daily life. Challenge yourself to step out of your comfort zone, try new behaviors, and cultivate a lifestyle of intentional growth and transformation.

7. Seek Guidance: Use the powerful, Visionary Prayers to invite God's perspective and presence into your transformative process. Don't just recite these words – let them ignite fires of faith. As you pray, let the Breath of God resuscitate dead places until promised realities burst forth. Keep contending until all opposing forces lie crushed beneath the majesty of Christ's Eternal Yes!

8. Connect with community: While this workbook can be completed independently, there is power in sharing your journey with others. Consider finding a trusted friend, mentor, or small group with whom you can discuss your insights, share your struggles, and pray for one another as you navigate the path of transformation together.

9. Revisit and review: Transformation is an ongoing process, and the insights and revelations you gain from this workbook may continue to unfold over time. Don't hesitate to revisit chapters, re-engage with the exercises, and continue to seek fresh revelation and application in your life.

Approach each exercise with a spirit of curiosity, creativity, and willingness to step outside your comfort zone. Remember that the goal is not perfection but progress and growth. Be patient with yourself, celebrate your breakthroughs, and trust that every small step is leading you closer to the person God created you to be.

CHAPTER 1

PERCEPTION, MY TRUTH

Our perceptions are shaped by a complex interplay of factors. The lenses through which we view ourselves and the world around us profoundly impact our thoughts, emotions, and behaviors, often in ways we may not even be aware of. When our perceptions are distorted or misaligned with reality, we can find ourselves feeling stuck, confused, or disconnected from our authentic selves and others. In this chapter, we'll explore the various influences that have shaped your unique perceptions and consider how gaining awareness of these lenses can lead to greater clarity, growth, and authenticity in your life. You'll also identify areas where your perceptions may be limiting or distorting your understanding and begin to challenge and reframe those beliefs with truth and grace.

Reflection Questions

1. How have your core values, family background, and life experiences shaped your perceptions and worldview?

_____

_____

_____

2. Describe a time you made an assumption about someone based on limited information. How did that impact your interaction with them?

_____

_____

_____

3. In what areas of your life do you think you might have distorted perceptions? How could you challenge those?

_____

_____

_____

Mirror Moment: Take an honest look at your self-perception. Journal about the messages you internalized about yourself growing up. How have those shaped the way you see yourself and move through the world today?

Transformative Insights: Reflect on a moment when you challenged a long-held belief or perception about yourself or your life circumstances.

1. How did this shift in perspective impact your thoughts, emotions, and actions moving forward?

_____

_____

_____

2. Consider how embracing a more fluid and growth-oriented mindset can open up new possibilities for personal transformation and self-discovery.

_____

_____

_____

Perception in Action: Set an intention to catch yourself making snap judgments or assumptions. When you notice it happening, pause and challenge yourself to consider alternative perspectives or gather more information before drawing conclusions.

Clarity Corner: Reflect on a situation where your initial perception of something turned out to be inaccurate or incomplete. What additional information shifted your perspective? How did that experience impact your approach moving forward?

_____

_____

_____

_____

Self-Awareness Exercise: Spend a day paying attention to your thoughts and reactions. Note any patterns or triggers that influence your perceptions.

Visionary Prayer: *Father, I ask for an impartation of Your divine perspective. heal any places where my perception has been distorted by pain or lies, and give me the courage to embrace Your perspective, even when it challenges my own. Give me eyes to see as You see and a heart to receive Your transformative revelation. In Jesus' name, Amen.*

CHAPTER 2

WHO AM I?

Our sense of identity is a core component of our human experience, shaping how we understand ourselves, relate to others, and move through the world. Our identities have been molded by a complex web of influences – from our families to the messages we've absorbed from society and culture to the experiences that have marked our lives in both positive and painful ways. It's easy to internalize labels, roles, and expectations that don't truly reflect the fullness of who we are, leading to a sense of confusion, disconnection, or inauthenticity. In this chapter, we'll explore the concept of identity through the lens of God's truth, examining the various factors that have shaped our sense of self and considering how you can anchor your identity in the unshakable reality of who God says you are. You'll begin to peel back the layers of false identity and step more fully into the joyful, purposeful life you were created for.

Reflection Questions

1. What family stories, traditions, or legacies have had the greatest influence on your identity and sense of self?

_____

_____

_____

2. Reflect on moments in your life when you felt misunderstood or pigeon-holed by others' perceptions of you. How did you respond? What did you learn about yourself?

_____

_____

_____

3. How has your understanding of your identity and purpose evolved over the years? What influences have shaped that?

_____

_____

_____

Mirror Moment: Write a letter to your younger self, offering wisdom, encouragement, and affirmation of her inherent worth and potential.

📖 **Transformative Insights:** Identify a limiting belief or self-defeating pattern that has held you back from fully embracing your authentic self.

1. Imagine how your life could change if you were to replace this belief with a more empowering and self-affirming truth.

_____

_____

_____

2. What steps can you take to begin embodying this new perspective and showing up more fully as the person you were created to be?

_____

_____

_____

🚶 **Perception in Action:** Identify three core values or character traits that you want to define your life and legacy. Look for opportunities to embody and express those qualities in your daily interactions.

💡 **Clarity Corner:** Visualize yourself at 90 years old, looking back on your life with satisfaction and gratitude. What do you want to be remembered for? How can you align your life now with that vision?

_____

_____

_____

_____

_____

🕯 **Affirmation Exercise:** Write 3 affirmations about your God-given identity, gifts and purpose. Place them where you'll see them daily.

🕯 **Visionary Prayer:** *Heavenly Father, I thank You for the truth of my identity in Christ. I declare that I am Your beloved child, created in Your image, redeemed by Your grace, and destined for Your purposes. Break off every false identity and let Your Spirit bear witness with my spirit that I belong to You. May my life be a reflection of Your glory and goodness. In Jesus' name, Amen.*

CHAPTER 3

PERCEPTION OF FAMILY

The families we grow up in are often our first and most formative experiences of the world, shaping our earliest beliefs, values, and patterns of relating. Whether our family dynamics were nurturing or neglectful, empowering or limiting, they left an indelible imprint on our hearts and minds, influencing how we see ourselves, others, and God. It's easy to absorb familial labels, roles, and expectations without question, internalizing messages that may not align with our true identities or callings. In this chapter, we'll explore the impact of family perceptions on your sense of self and your relationships, examining the ways in which your unique family system has both blessed and challenged you. You'll also identify patterns of strength and struggle in your family lineage and prayerfully discern how you want to build on the positive legacies while breaking free from the limiting cycles.

Reflection Questions

1. How have comparisons to siblings or other family members (positive or negative) impacted your self-perception over the years?

_____

_____

_____

2. In what ways have you internalized family labels, roles or expectations? How do those shape your view of yourself today?

_____

_____

_____

3. Reflect on a family member who has positively influenced your life. What qualities do you most admire in them? How could you cultivate those traits in yourself?

_____

_____

_____

Mirror Moment: Create a visual family tree, noting strengths, challenges, and patterns through the generations. Reflect on how you want to build on the positive and break any negative cycles.

📖 **Transformative Insights:** Reflect on a family dynamic or pattern that has significantly shaped your own perceptions and behaviors.

1. Consider how gaining a deeper understanding and compassion for your family members' experiences and perspectives can help you break free from unhelpful cycles and forge a new path forward.

_____

_____

_____

2. What would it look like to approach your family relationships with greater empathy, curiosity, and intention?

_____

_____

_____

🚶 **Perception in Action:** Initiate a conversation with a family member you've had tension or unresolved issues with. Approach the interaction with empathy, curiosity, and a desire to understand their perspective and experience.

💡 **Clarity Corner:** Identify a limiting belief or pattern you've inherited from your family of origin. What would it look like to rewrite that script and establish a new narrative for your lineage?

_____

_____

_____

_____

🍴 **Family Tree Exercise:** Create a visual family tree, noting strengths, challenges and patterns through the generations. Reflect on how you want to build on the positive and break any negative cycles.

🙏 **Visionary Prayer:** *Gracious God, I thank You for the gift of family and the unique story You are writing through our lives. I ask for Your wisdom and revelation to perceive my family through Your eyes of love and redemption. Where there is brokenness, bring healing. Where there is division, bring reconciliation. Use our family to display Your faithfulness for generations to come. In Jesus' name, Amen.*

CHAPTER 4

PERCEPTIONS OF OTHERS

Just as our self-perceptions are shaped by a complex interplay of influences and experiences, so too are our perceptions of others. The lenses through which we view the people around us – whether family members, friends, colleagues, or strangers – are colored by our own biases, assumptions, and past experiences. These perceptions can have a profound impact on our relationships and interactions, often in ways we may not even be aware of. In this chapter, we'll explore the various factors that shape our perceptions of others, from our early familial patterns to our cultural conditioning to our own unhealed wounds and fears. You'll have the opportunity to identify your own biases and blind spots and to practice seeing others through the eyes of compassion and curiosity.

Reflection Questions

1. Recall a time you felt unfairly judged by someone's words or actions towards you. How did that make you feel? How did you respond?

_____

_____

_____

2. Reflect on an instance where your own biases or preconceived notions negatively colored your perception of someone else. What did you learn from that?

_____

_____

_____

3. How do you typically respond when you feel misunderstood – retreat inward, lash out, try to explain yourself? Is there a more constructive way you could engage?

_____

_____

_____

Mirror Moment: Journal about a relationship or interaction that has been strained by misperceptions or assumptions. What would it look like to approach that situation with a posture of grace and understanding?

Transformative Insights: Recall a time when you made a snap judgment about someone based on limited information or preconceived notions.

1. How did this impact your interaction with them and your overall perception of their character?

_____

_____

_____

2. Reflect on the transformative power of leading with curiosity, openness, and a willingness to see beyond surface-level assumptions.

_____

_____

_____

Perception in Action: Challenge yourself to have a conversation with someone you've made assumptions about based on limited information. Approach the interaction with openness and a genuine desire to understand their story.

Clarity Corner: Identify a group of people you tend to stereotype or make generalizations about. Research or seek out personal stories to gain a more nuanced, humanized perspective on their experiences.

_____

_____

_____

_____

_____

Letter-Writing Exercise: Write a letter to someone who has hurt you through their judgments or negative perceptions (you don't have to send it). Express your feelings and release the pain to God.

Visionary Prayer: *God of Love, I pray for a baptism of Your compassion and kindness to flood my heart. Remove the filters of judgment and criticism, and give me eyes to see the gold in others. May my life be marked by Jesus' empathy and grace, drawing people into encounters with Your transformative love. Let me be a conduit of Your acceptance and mercy. In Jesus' name, Amen.*

CHAPTER 5

TRANSITION FROM A GIRL TO A WOMAN

The journey from girlhood to womanhood is marked by profound physical, emotional, and spiritual changes. During this time, our perceptions of ourselves, our relationships, and our place in the world undergo significant shifts, shaping our identities. We may absorb messages from family, friends, and society about what it means to be a woman – messages that can either empower us or limit us. In this chapter, we'll explore the unique challenges and opportunities of adolescence and consider how our experiences have impacted our sense of self and our relationships. We'll also identify the gifts and strengths that emerged during this time and explore how we can continue to cultivate them in our lives today.

Reflection Questions

1. What messages did you receive about sexuality and intimate relationships growing up? How have those impacted your experiences and choices as an adult?

_____

_____

_____

2. Reflect on your own journey through adolescence. What were the most challenging aspects for you personally? The most joyful? What do you know now that you wish your teenage self understood?

_____

_____

_____

3. How have your friendships with other women evolved over the years? What traits do you most value in your female friendships?

_____

_____

_____

Mirror Moment: Write a letter of encouragement to a younger girl in your life who is navigating the challenges of growing up. Share the wisdom and insights you've gained from your own journey.

📖 **Transformative Insights:** Identify a key lesson or insight you gained during your own journey of transitioning from girlhood to womanhood.

1. How has this understanding shaped your sense of self, your relationships, and your path in life?

_____

_____

_____

2. Consider how embracing the wisdom and growth born from this transformative period can continue to guide and empower you as you navigate future challenges and opportunities.

_____

_____

_____

🏃 **Perception in Action:** Identify a woman you admire who embodies authentic femininity and lives out her purpose with courage and grace. Reach out to her and express your appreciation or ask if you can treat her to coffee and glean some of her wisdom.

💡 **Clarity Corner:** Reflect on the expectations and pressures society places on women to fit certain molds or play certain roles. How have you internalized those messages? What would it look like to define your own womanhood based on God's truth?

_____

_____

_____

_____

🍽 **Coming-of-Age Reflection:** Write about a defining "coming of age" moment or season for you. What made it significant? How did it shape your journey into womanhood?

🕎 **Visionary Prayer:** *Almighty God, I thank You for the sacred journey of womanhood. Heal the places where I have felt ashamed, confused, or inadequate. Break off the limitations and labels and call forth the fullness of my identity as a daughter of the King. May I rise into the strength, dignity, purpose, and destiny You have ordained for me. May I be a light to other women on the path to wholeness. In Jesus' name, Amen.*

CHAPTER 6

THE WOMAN WITH THE ISSUE

Physical and emotional suffering can have a profound impact on our perceptions of ourselves, our lives, and our faith. When we face chronic illness, pain, or other health challenges, it's easy to feel like our bodies have betrayed us, or that we are somehow less valuable or capable than we once were. We may struggle with feelings of isolation, frustration, and even despair, wondering where God is amid our trials. In this chapter, we'll explore the ways in which suffering can shape our identities and worldviews and how we can find hope, meaning, and purpose even in the hardest of seasons. You'll have the opportunity to process your own experiences of physical and emotional pain and to cultivate a deeper sense of trust and intimacy with God in the midst of suffering.

Reflection Questions

1. How has struggling with a health issue (mental, emotional or physical) changed your perception of yourself and your capabilities? In what ways has it made you stronger?

_____

_____

_____

2. Reflect on a dark time you've gone through. How did you experience God's presence even in the midst of pain and questioning? What scriptures or spiritual truths sustained you?

_____

_____

_____

3. What stigmas or shame have you encountered related to your health struggles? How could you challenge those, both internally and externally?

_____

_____

_____

Mirror Moment: Write a letter to your body, expressing gratitude for its resilience and offering compassion and care for the ways it's suffered.

Transformative Insights: Reflect on a time when you faced a significant personal struggle or challenge that tested your faith and resilience.

1. What unexpected strengths, insights, or opportunities for growth emerged from this difficult experience?

_____

_____

_____

2. How can you apply these transformative lessons to other areas of your life, and use your story to inspire and encourage others facing similar trials?

_____

_____

_____

Perception in Action: Connect with someone else who shares your health struggle. Offer them empathy, encouragement, and the reminder that they are not alone.

Clarity Corner: Reflect on how your experience of suffering has deepened your capacity for compassion and empathy. How can you use your pain as a platform to minister to others?

_____

_____

_____

_____

Self-Compassion Exercise: Write yourself a compassionate, encouraging letter as you would to a dear friend going through a health battle. Speak words of empathy, resilience and hope.

Visionary Prayer: *Healing God, I bring my pain and suffering before You, trusting in Your power to restore and redeem. I declare that Your purposes are greater than my circumstances and that You are working all things together for my good. Give me eyes to see Your hand in the midst of the trials and a heart to receive Your comfort and strength. Use my story to bring hope and healing to others. In Jesus' name, Amen.*

CHAPTER 7

SELF-REFLECTION

The practice of self-reflection is an essential component of personal growth, emotional healing, and spiritual transformation. When we take the time to honestly examine our thoughts, feelings, and behaviors, we gain a deeper understanding of ourselves and the factors that shape our perceptions and experiences. In this chapter, we'll explore the power of self-reflection as a tool for cultivating self-awareness, authenticity, and wholeness. You'll have the opportunity to delve into your own inner world with courage and curiosity, uncovering both the beauty and the brokenness within.

Reflection Questions

1. What insecurities or past hurts do you still need to address in order to see yourself as God sees you – forgiven, beloved, and made new?

_____

_____

_____

2. Reflect on the coping mechanisms you've used to avoid dealing with painful truths about yourself or your story. How have they helped or hindered your growth?

_____

_____

_____

3. What practices of self-reflection and self-awareness resonate with you and help you gain clarity – journaling, prayer, therapy, etc.? How could you incorporate them more into your life?

_____

_____

_____

_____

Mirror Moment: Write a confession, either to God or a trusted friend, acknowledging the areas of your life where you've struggled to be honest with yourself. Receive the grace and forgiveness that is freely offered.

Transformative Insights: Identify a blind spot or area of personal growth that has been revealed to you through the practice of self-reflection.

1. What steps can you take to address this growth edge with courage, compassion, and intentionality?

_____

_____

_____

2. Consider how cultivating a habit of regular self-reflection can support your ongoing personal and spiritual transformation.

_____

_____

_____

Perception in Action: Set aside 20 minutes for a "brain dump" journaling session. Write down every thought and feeling that comes to mind, without judgment or filter. Notice any recurring themes or patterns and prayerfully consider what they might be revealing about your current state.

Clarity Corner: Identify a past version of yourself that you need to make peace with – perhaps a younger self who made mistakes or suffered trauma. Write a letter of compassion and understanding to that part of you, extending the grace and acceptance you'd offer a beloved friend.

_____

_____

_____

_____

_____

Forgiveness Meditation: Visualize yourself at different ages and stages of life. Offer each version of yourself compassion, empathy and forgiveness. Receive God's grace for your whole story.

Visionary Prayer: *God of Wisdom, I invite Your searching gaze to penetrate the depths of my soul. Shine Your light into every hidden place and expose what needs to be brought into alignment with Your truth. Give me the courage to face myself honestly and the humility to receive Your transformative grace. May I become a pure vessel for Your glory. In Jesus' name, Amen.*

CHAPTER 8

FACT OR FICTION

In an age of information overload and competing worldviews, discerning truth from falsehood can be a daunting task. Our perceptions of reality are shaped not only by our personal experiences and beliefs but also by the messages we absorb from media, culture, and the people around us. It's easy to mistake opinions for facts, to cling to comfortable narratives even when they don't align with reality, or to fall prey to misinformation and manipulation. In this chapter, we'll explore the importance of developing discernment and a commitment to truth-seeking. We'll examine the various factors that shape our perceptions of truth, from confirmation bias to echo chambers to the influence of power and privilege. You'll have the opportunity to identify your own assumptions and blind spots and to practice the skills of critical thinking, fact-checking, and open-minded inquiry.

Reflection Questions

1. When have you mistaken your subjective perspective as objective truth? What resulted from imposing your view on others as fact rather than opinion?

_____

_____

_____

2. Reflect on a time you made an erroneous snap judgment about a person or situation. What did you later come to understand more fully? How did you rectify your misperception?

_____

_____

_____

3. In what situations do you find it most challenging to discern between fact and perception? How could trusted outside input provide clarity?

_____

_____

_____

Mirror Moment: Journal about a belief or perspective you hold strongly. Examine the influences and experiences that have shaped that view. Consider how someone with a different background or lens might perceive the same issue.

Transformative Insights: Reflect on a time when you discovered that a long-held belief or perception was based on incomplete or inaccurate information.

1. How did this realization shift your understanding and approach moving forward?

_____

_____

_____

2. What strategies can you employ to discern truth more effectively and make well-informed decisions in various areas of your life?

_____

_____

_____

Perception in Action: Commit to fact-checking a news article or social media post before reacting to it or sharing it with others. Model responsible media consumption and encourage critical thinking in your sphere of influence.

Clarity Corner: Reflect on a time you changed your mind about a significant issue or belief. What new information or experiences shifted your perspective? How did it feel to admit you were wrong or had more to learn?

_____

_____

_____

_____

_____

Media Literacy Exercise: Analyze a news article, opinion piece or social media post. Identify any statements presented as facts vs. opinions. Note any loaded language or bias.

Visionary Prayer: *God of Truth, in a world of confusion and deception, I choose to anchor my life in the unshakable foundation of Your Word. Give me a discerning mind and a heart that seeks after wisdom. Help me to pursue truth with humility and grace, and to be a vessel of Your love and righteousness in every sphere of my life. In Jesus' name, Amen.*

CHAPTER 9

EMPATHY AND GRACE IN THE WORKPLACE

We are called to bring compassion, understanding, and wisdom into our workplace. Whether you are a manager, a service provider, or a collaborator, you can create an environment where people feel seen, heard, and valued. By extending grace and empathy in the face of difficult situations and diverse personalities, you can foster a culture of trust, respect, and belonging that brings out the best in everyone.

Reflection Questions

1. In your professional life, when have you struggled to extend grace and compassion to a colleague, client, or supervisor who didn't meet your expectations or live up to their initial impression?

_____

_____

_____

2. Reflect on how your family of origin has shaped your understanding of emotional boundaries and availability in the workplace. In what ways do you want to grow in offering empathy and understanding to others professionally?

_____

_____

_____

3. Recall a time when you felt truly seen, heard, and valued in your work environment. What did your colleague or supervisor do to create an atmosphere of empathy and non-judgment? How can you cultivate those qualities in your own professional relationships?

_____

_____

_____

Mirror Moment: Journal about a recent interaction or project at work that challenged your patience, compassion, or professionalism. What personal triggers or biases might have influenced your response? How can you process those reactions in a healthy way and approach future situations with greater wisdom and grace?

Transformative Insights: Reflect on a moment when extending empathy, compassion, or forgiveness in your workplace led to a breakthrough in communication, collaboration, or conflict resolution.

1. What did that experience teach you about the transformative power of grace and understanding in professional settings?

_____

_____

_____

2. How can you apply those insights to foster a more positive, productive, and empowering work culture?

_____

_____

_____

Perception in Action: Identify someone with whom you have experienced tension, misunderstanding, or conflict. Commit to initiating a conversation with them this week, focusing on listening to understand their perspective and experiences. Approach the dialogue with curiosity, humility, and a desire to find common ground and build connection.

Clarity Corner: Reflect on the ethical principles and best practices in your field. How do they align with your personal values and beliefs? What would it look like to integrate your faith and professional identity in a way that feels authentic and ethical?

_____

_____

_____

_____

Empathy in Action: Choose a day this week to practice active listening and empathy in all your workplace interactions. Pay attention to verbal and nonverbal cues, reflect on what you hear, and seek to understand each person's unique perspective and experience. Journal about how this practice impacts your relationships, communication, and overall job satisfaction.

Visionary Prayer: *Father, I dedicate my work to You, asking that You would grant me the patience to navigate difficult conversations and situations with skill and empathy and the humility to recognize my own limitations and biases. Help me to be a catalyst for positive change and an agent of reconciliation. Empower me to serve with excellence, integrity, and love. In Jesus' name. Amen.*

CHAPTER 10

PERMISSION TO RESPECT PERSPECTIVE

In an increasingly polarized world, the ability to engage with different viewpoints is imperative. This requires the humility to listen, the courage to empathize, and the wisdom to discern truth in the midst of competing perspectives. In this chapter, we'll explore the challenges and opportunities of respecting perspectives and consider how this practice can deepen our relationships and expand our understanding. You'll have the opportunity to practice the skills of active listening, perspective-taking, and dialogue across differences.

Reflection Questions

1. When have you felt defensive or threatened by an opinion or belief different from your own? How can you practice listening and respecting others' perspectives even when you disagree?

_____

_____

_____

2. Reflect on people in your life with backgrounds and experiences very different from yours. What could you learn from engaging with them and seeking to understand their point of view?

_____

_____

_____

3. Think of a divisive issue about which you hold a strong view. Challenge yourself to articulate the other side's perspective as generously and fairly as possible. What common ground can you find?

_____

_____

_____

_____

Mirror Moment: Journal about a time you felt heard and respected in sharing a divergent or unpopular opinion. What made that interaction feel safe and productive, even if the other person disagreed with you?

Transformative Insights: Identify a relationship or situation in which honoring and respecting diverse perspectives has led to greater understanding, collaboration, or positive change.

1. What key principles or practices supported this outcome, and how can you apply them more broadly in your life?

_____

_____

_____

2. Consider the transformative potential of approaching differences with curiosity, humility, and a commitment to finding common ground.

_____

_____

_____

Perception in Action: Seek out a book, podcast, or perspective on an issue you care about from someone with a very different lived experience or ideological background. Approach it with a learning posture and reflect on what new insights or questions it raises for you.

Clarity Corner: Reflect on how your own identities, privileges, and experiences shape your lens on certain issues. What blind spots or assumptions might you need to challenge in order to engage more empathetically with others?

_____

_____

_____

_____

Perspective-Taking Exercise: Choose a book, movie or show that portrays a perspective very different from your own lived experience. Consume it with an open, learning posture. Process what stood out to you and shifted your understanding.

Visionary Prayer: *God of Peace, I pray for a spirit of humility and understanding to navigate the complexities of differing perspectives. Give me the grace to listen with an open heart and the discernment to recognize Your truth in every encounter. May my life be a bridge of reconciliation, bringing unity and healing to a divided world. Let Your Kingdom come, and Your will be done. In Jesus' name, Amen.*

CHAPTER 11

PERCEPTION POST-TRAUMA

Trauma can alter our brain chemistry, nervous system, and fundamental sense of trust and safety. It can leave us feeling hypervigilant, emotionally reactive, and disconnected from our own bodies and experiences. Trauma can also distort our perceptions of reality, leading us to view ourselves as broken or defective, others as dangerous or untrustworthy, and the world as unpredictable or threatening. In this chapter, we'll explore the impact of trauma and consider how the journey of healing and recovery can help us reclaim a sense of wholeness, agency, and connection. You'll have the opportunity to process your own experiences of trauma and develop a personalized plan for self-care and support.

Reflection Questions ?

1. What past wounds still impact how you engage in relationships today? Identify how those unhealed hurts may be subconsciously influencing your perceptions and interactions.

_____

_____

_____

_____

2. Reflect on the subtle lies trauma has led you to believe about your worth, lovability, and future. Counter them with specific truths that affirm your value and potential.

_____

_____

_____

3. Who are the safe people you can process your healing journey with? How can you invite them to support you and speak truth when your perceptions feel distorted?

_____

_____

_____

Mirror Moment: Write a compassionate letter to a part of yourself that is still carrying pain or fear from a past trauma. Offer that wounded part understanding, validation, and reassurance of your commitment to healing.

Transformative Insights: Identify a key insight or revelation that has emerged from your own journey of healing and growth in the aftermath of trauma.

1. How has this understanding shifted your perception of yourself, your experiences, and your path forward?

_____

_____

_____

2. What wisdom can you draw from your own process of post-traumatic growth to support and inspire others on their healing journeys?

_____

_____

_____

Perception in Action: Identify a trigger or situation that often causes you to react from a place of trauma or fear. Develop a safety plan or coping strategy to help you respond with greater self-compassion and groundedness.

Clarity Corner: Reflect on the story of someone you admire who has navigated trauma or adversity with resilience and grace. What can you learn from their journey and apply to your own healing process?

_____

_____

_____

_____

_____

Grounding Technique: When you feel emotionally triggered or overwhelmed, practice a grounding technique to calm your nervous system and allow your rational brain to re-engage. Try box breathing, progressive muscle relaxation or engaging your 5 senses.

Visionary Prayer: _God of Restoration, I bring my wounded heart and shattered memories before You, declaring that no darkness is too deep for Your light to penetrate. I pray for a divine rewiring of my mind and emotions, breaking the power of trauma and establishing new pathways of peace. Anoint me with the oil of joy and clothe me with a garment of praise. May my testimony be a catalyst for healing and hope. In Jesus' name, Amen._

CHAPTER 12

THE POWER OF VULNERABILITY

In a world that often equates vulnerability with weakness, embracing vulnerability can be a radical act of faith and courage. As we navigate the journey of self-discovery and transformation, we are invited to confront our deepest fears, insecurities, and shame. This process of uncovering and surrendering the hidden parts of ourselves is not for the faint of heart, but it is the path to true freedom, wholeness, and authentic connection. In this chapter, we will explore the transformative power of vulnerability and its role in our spiritual, emotional, and relational growth. As we learn to show up authentically in our lives and relationships, we open ourselves to the healing, restoration, and intimacy that God desires for us.

Reflection Questions ?

1. In what areas of your life do you find it most challenging to be vulnerable? What fears or beliefs hold you back from authenticity in these spaces?

_____

_____

_____

2. Reflect on a time when you witnessed someone else's vulnerability and felt inspired or moved by their courage. What did you learn from their example?

_____

_____

_____

3. How has your understanding of vulnerability evolved throughout your life? What experiences or insights have shifted your perspective on the value of being vulnerable?

_____

_____

_____

_____

Mirror Moment: Write a letter to a younger version of yourself who struggled with vulnerability. Offer words of compassion, encouragement, and wisdom from your current perspective.

Transformative Insights: Reflect on a time when you took a risk to be vulnerable and authentic in a relationship or situation.

1. What fears or barriers did you have to overcome, and what growth or deepening of connection resulted from this courageous act?

_____

_____

_____

2. How can you leverage the power of vulnerability to create more intimacy, trust, and transformation in your life and relationships?

_____

_____

_____

Perception in Action: Identify one relationship or setting where you want to practice greater vulnerability. Take a small step this week to share more of your authentic self in that space, and notice how it impacts your connection and growth.

Clarity Corner: Reflect on a time when you took a risk to be vulnerable and experienced positive results. What did you learn about the power of vulnerability through that experience?

_____

_____

_____

_____

_____

Vulnerability Exercise: Share a personal struggle or insecurity with a trusted friend or mentor. Practice letting yourself be seen and supported in your vulnerability.

Visionary Prayer: *Lord, I choose to embrace the power of vulnerability as an avenue for deep connection and transformation. I break agreement with shame and fear, and I step into the light of Your love. Give me the courage to be fully seen and known, trusting that my weaknesses will become a platform for Your strength. May my authenticity be a invitation for others to find wholeness in You. In Jesus' name, Amen.*

When we feel misperceived, it can stir up feelings of frustration, loneliness, and even shame. We may question our own worth or feel pressure to hide or change parts of ourselves to fit others' expectations. Over time, the weight of being misunderstood can erode our sense of self and our willingness to show up authentically in our relationships and communities. In this chapter, we'll explore the pain of being misunderstood and the power of reclaiming our own narratives and truths. You'll have the opportunity to process your experiences of being misunderstood and to practice the skills of self-awareness, assertiveness, and boundary-setting.

Reflection Questions ❓

1. When do you find yourself most tempted to hide or tamp down your authentic self for fear of being misunderstood? What would it look like to show up vulnerably as you are?

_____

_____

_____

2. Reflect on the cost of constantly shape-shifting to meet others' expectations. How has that habit impacted your ability to feel truly known and loved? What boundaries could you set to protect your wellbeing?

_____

_____

_____

3. If you gave yourself radical permission to be fully authentic, what parts of yourself would you express more freely? How do you want to be experienced by others?

_____

_____

_____

Mirror Moment: Write an "I am" poem celebrating the unique facets of your personality, passions, and purpose. Share it with a trusted friend or read it aloud to yourself as an act of self-affirmation.

Transformative Insights: Reflect on a time when you felt deeply misunderstood or mischaracterized by others.

1. What did this experience reveal about your own sense of self and the importance of living authentically?

_____

_____

_____

2. Consider how developing a strong foundation of self-awareness, self-compassion, and self-acceptance can help you navigate the challenges of being misunderstood with greater resilience and grace.

_____

_____

_____

Perception in Action: Practice communicating your needs, feelings, and boundaries clearly and directly with someone you trust. Notice how it feels to express yourself authentically, even if it feels vulnerable or awkward at first.

Clarity Corner: Reflect on a time you made an assumption or judgment about someone else that was later challenged or disproven. What did that experience teach you about the limits of your own perceptions and the importance of seeking to understand others' authentic selves?

_____

_____

_____

_____

Authentic Communication Exercise: Before your next vulnerable conversation, take time to journal about what you want to express and why it matters to you. Pray for the courage to communicate honestly and the wisdom to do so lovingly.

Visionary Prayer: *God of Comfort, I thank You that You see me, know me, and understand me completely. When I face misunderstanding or rejection, remind me that my identity and worth are found in You alone. Give me the grace to communicate with clarity and love. Give me the discernment to cultivate relationships that honor the fullness of who I am. May I find rest and belonging in Your unchanging acceptance. In Jesus' name, Amen.*

Grief and loss are an inevitable part of the human experience, touching every life at some point in the journey. Whether it is the loss of a loved one, the end of a relationship, the shattering of a dream, or the collective grief of a hurting world, the pain of loss can feel overwhelming, disorienting, and isolating. In these moments, we may find ourselves grappling with profound questions of faith, purpose, and identity as we seek to make sense of the broken pieces of our lives. In this chapter, we will navigate grief and loss through the lens of faith and self-discovery. We will discover how to find hope, meaning, and purpose even in the darkest of seasons.

Reflection Questions ?

1. What losses have you experienced that have significantly impacted your life? How have those losses shaped your perception of yourself, others, and the world?

_____

_____

_____

2. Reflect on a time when you tried to avoid or numb the pain of grief. What were the consequences of that avoidance? What did you learn about the importance of facing and processing painful emotions?

_____

_____

_____

_____

3. How has your faith influenced your understanding and experience of grief? What biblical truths or spiritual practices have brought you comfort and hope in times of loss?

_____

_____

_____

Mirror Moment: Write a letter to someone you have lost, expressing your feelings, sharing your memories, and entrusting them to God's eternal care.

Transformative Insights: Identify a meaningful lesson or insight you have gained through your own experiences of grief and loss.

1. How has this understanding shaped your perspective on life, love, and the preciousness of each moment?

_____

_____

_____

2. What practices or rituals have supported your healing process, and how can you draw upon this wisdom to find comfort, hope, and resilience in the face of future challenges?

_____

_____

_____

Perception in Action: Reach out to someone who is grieving with a note of encouragement, an act of service, or an offer to listen. Put yourself in their shoes and consider what would be most meaningful to you in a time of loss.

Clarity Corner: Identify a loss that you are still processing. What stage of grief do you find yourself in – denial, anger, bargaining, depression, acceptance? What do you need to help you move towards healing and hope?

_____

_____

_____

_____

_____

Mourning Ritual: Create a meaningful way to honor a significant loss, such as journaling memories, making a photo collage, or donating to a related cause. Invite God into this sacred space.

Visionary Prayer: *Comforting God, I entrust my grief and pain to You, believing that You see me, You know me, and You weep with me. Help me face my losses with honesty and courage. Help me to trust in Your promise to redeem every tear and heartache for Your glory. Minister to me by Your Spirit and lead me into the spacious place of healing and hope. In Jesus' name, Amen.*

CHAPTER 15

THE ROLE OF MENTORSHIP

Mentorship is a powerful catalyst for growth, transformation, and impact. Mentors' have shaped countless individuals' lives, helping them discover their unique purpose, navigate challenges and opportunities, and realize their full potential. The presence of mentors who believe in us, challenge us, and invest in our growth can make all the difference in our personal, professional, and spiritual development. In this chapter, we will explore the crucial role of mentorship and discover how to cultivate successful mentoring relationships that empower us to thrive.

Reflection Questions

1. Who have been the most influential mentors in your life – personally, professionally, or spiritually? What qualities made their guidance so meaningful and transformative?

_____

_____

_____

2. Reflect on a time when you have had the opportunity to mentor or pour into someone else. What did that experience teach you about leadership, service, and investing in others?

_____

_____

_____

3. What areas of your life could benefit most from the wisdom and support of a mentor right now? What kind of guidance and accountability would help you grow into the next version of yourself?

_____

_____

_____

_____

Mirror Moment: Write a letter of gratitude to a mentor who has significantly impacted your life. Share how their influence has shaped you and express your appreciation for their investment.

Transformative Insights: Reflect on a mentoring relationship that has significantly impacted your personal or professional growth.

1. What key qualities or actions made this relationship so transformative, and how have you internalized these lessons in your own life and leadership?

_____

_____

_____

2. Consider how you can pay forward the gift of mentorship by seeking opportunities to guide, support, and empower others on their journeys.

_____

_____

_____

Perception in Action: Identify someone in your sphere of influence who could benefit from your experience and support. Reach out and offer to connect over coffee or Zoom. Come prepared to listen well and to share your story with vulnerability and authenticity.

Clarity Corner: Reflect on a key lesson or piece of advice you have received from a mentor. How has that wisdom impacted your perspective and choices? Consider how you can pay that insight forward to someone else.

_____

_____

_____

_____

Mentorship Reflection: Journal about the kind of mentor you would like to become. What values, skills, and experiences do you want to pass on? How can you start preparing now to be that person?

Visionary Prayer: _Wise and Loving God, thank You for the gift of mentors who have poured into my life. Help me to receive their wisdom with humility and to apply it with courage and faithfulness. Show me how to steward this gift by investing in others so that I may leave a legacy of faith and fruitfulness. Multiply Your Kingdom through these divine connections. In Jesus' name, Amen._

CHAPTER 16

TRUTH PREVAILS

In a world that often blurs the lines between perception and reality, the pursuit of truth can feel like a daunting and even dangerous endeavor. Competing narratives, ideologies, and agendas vie for our attention and allegiance, often leaving us confused, disoriented, and divided. In the face of such challenges, it can be tempting to retreat into the safety of our own echo chambers or to resign ourselves to a relativistic worldview that denies the existence of objective truth altogether. Yet, we are called to be seekers and speakers of truth, even when it is unpopular, uncomfortable, or costly.

Reflection Questions ?

1. In what areas of your life or relationships do you find it most challenging to live with transparency and authenticity? What fears or insecurities hold you back from fully embracing your truth?

_____

_____

_____

2. Reflect on a time when you witnessed the power of truth to bring freedom, healing, or transformation. What did that experience teach you about the importance of living with integrity and honesty?

_____

_____

_____

3. How has your understanding of God's truth evolved throughout your faith journey? What spiritual practices or disciplines help you stay grounded in the truth of who you are in Christ?

_____

_____

_____

Mirror Moment: Write a declaration of your identity in Christ, anchoring your sense of self in the unshakable truths of God's Word. Speak this over yourself daily as an act of faith and self-acceptance.

Transformative Insights: Identify a moment when speaking or living your truth required significant courage and conviction.

1. What internal and external obstacles did you have to overcome, and what growth or liberation resulted from this act of authenticity?

_____

_____

_____

2. Reflect on the transformative power of aligning your life with your deepest values and truths, even in the face of challenge or resistance.

_____

_____

_____

Perception in Action: Identify a relationship or situation in which you have been tempted to hide or compromise your truth. Prayerfully consider how you can begin to communicate with greater transparency and authenticity while still extending grace and wisdom.

Clarity Corner: Reflect on a biblical figure who exemplified the power of living in truth, even in the face of opposition or adversity (e.g., Daniel, Esther, Paul). What can you learn from their example of courage, conviction, and faith?

_____

_____

_____

_____

Truth Affirmation: Write a personal manifesto or anthem that declares your commitment to living with authenticity, integrity, and alignment with God's truth. Display it somewhere prominent as a daily reminder.

Visionary Prayer: *Faithful God, You are the way, the truth, and the life. Anchor my identity and purpose in the unshakable foundation of Your Word. Expose any areas of deceit or compromise in my life, and lead me in the path of integrity and authenticity. May my life be a testament to the liberating power of Your truth, drawing others into the freedom and wholeness You desire for us all. In Jesus' name, Amen.*

Transformation is not a one-time event but an ongoing adventure of growth, discovery, and surrender as we learn to partner with God's grace and power in every area of our lives. It is the work of the Holy Spirit within us, renewing our minds, healing our wounds, and empowering us to live out the fullness of our identity and calling. In this chapter, we will explore the power of transformation and its central role in our spiritual, emotional, and relational flourishing. We will discover how to cooperate with the Holy Spirit and experience the abundant life that Jesus promised.

Reflection Questions

1. Reflect on a transformative experience or season in your life. What shifted in your perceptions, beliefs, or behaviors as a result? What did that process teach you about change and growth?

_____

_____

_____

2. What old patterns, habits, or mindsets do you feel God inviting you to release in order to step into the next version of yourself? What new ways of thinking or being is He calling you to embrace?

_____

_____

_____

_____

3. How have you seen the power of small, consistent actions over time to create meaningful transformation? What "little by little" steps can you take to keep growing and changing?

_____

_____

_____

Mirror Moment: Write a letter from your future self, 10 years from now. Imagine the person you have become and the transformation you have experienced. What wisdom and encouragement does that future self have for you now?

Transformative Insights: Reflect on a transformative experience or season in your life that catalyzed significant growth, healing, or change.

1. What key factors or practices supported this transformation, and how have you integrated these lessons into your ongoing journey of personal and spiritual evolution?

_____

_____

_____

2. Consider how you can continue to cultivate a mindset and lifestyle of continuous transformation and growth.

_____

_____

_____

Perception in Action: Identify a limiting belief or self-defeating pattern that you want to break free from. Replace it with a biblical truth or affirmation, and commit to speaking that truth over yourself daily.

Clarity Corner: Reflect on a biblical figure who experienced significant transformation (e.g. Paul, Moses, Mary Magdalene). What can you learn from their encounter with God and their journey of change?

_____

_____

_____

_____

_____

Transformation Timeline: Create a timeline of your life, marking significant moments of change, growth, and breakthrough. Celebrate the transformation you have already experienced and anticipate the new things God has in store.

Visionary Prayer: *Redeeming God, I'm thankful that You are always at work in my life, conforming me to the image of Christ. I surrender to the transformative power of Your Spirit, inviting You to reshape every aspect of my being. Break off the old patterns and mindsets, so that I may embrace all that You have for me. May my life be a living testimony of Your ability to bring beauty from ashes. In Jesus' name, Amen.*

True wholeness requires an integrated approach that honors the interdependence of our physical, psychological, and spiritual selves. In this chapter, we will explore the vital intersection of spirituality and mental health and discover how our faith can inform our understanding and experience of mental wellness. We will examine the practical ways that we can integrate our spiritual practices and beliefs with evidence-based strategies for mental health.

Reflection Questions ❓

1. How has your spiritual life impacted your mental and emotional well-being – both positively and negatively? What practices or beliefs have been most influential in your overall health?

_____

_____

_____

2. Reflect on a time when you wrestled with deep questions of faith and meaning in the midst of personal struggle. How did that experience shape your perception of God and your understanding of yourself?

_____

_____

_____

_____

3. In what areas of your life do you feel the tension between your public persona and your private struggles? How can you cultivate greater authenticity and congruence between your inner and outer life?

_____

_____

_____

Mirror Moment: Write a letter to God, expressing your deepest fears, doubts, and desires in your journey of spiritual and mental health. Offer your whole self to Him, trusting in His unconditional love and acceptance.

Transformative Insights: Reflect on a moment when you experienced a profound sense of wholeness, healing, or transformation through the integration of your spiritual practices and mental health care.

1. What key insights or revelations emerged from this experience about the interconnectedness of your mind, body, and spirit?

_____

_____

_____

2. How can you continue to cultivate a holistic approach to well-being that honors all aspects of your being?

_____

_____

_____

Perception in Action: Identify a spiritual discipline or practice that you want to incorporate into your daily routine for mental and emotional health (e.g. gratitude journaling, breath prayer, Scripture meditation). Commit to trying it out for a week and notice how it impacts your overall well-being.

Clarity Corner: Reflect on a spiritual mentor, leader, or figure who embodies the integration of deep faith and authentic humanity. What qualities or practices do you admire in their life and witness? How can you learn from their example and apply their wisdom to your own journey of spiritual and mental health?

_____

_____

_____

_____

Spiritual Self-Care Plan: Create a daily or weekly self-care plan that incorporates both spiritual practices and mental health strategies. Consider including activities such as prayer, meditation, journaling, creative expression, physical movement, and time in nature. Reflect on how each element supports your overall well-being and fosters a sense of connection to yourself, others, and God.

Visionary Prayer: *Creator God, I thank You for the intricate design of my mind, body and spirit, woven together in divine unity. Teach me to steward my mental health with wisdom and to cultivate a lifestyle of intimacy with You. May my life be a living testimony of Your power to restore and renew. In Jesus' name, Amen.*

CHAPTER 19

EMBRACING THE JOURNEY WITHIN

We live in a society that encourages us to look outside ourselves for meaning, purpose, and fulfillment. Yet, the most transformative journey is the one that takes us inward – where we can discover the truth of who we are and who we are meant to be. In this chapter, we will discover the tools, practices, and perspectives that can guide us on the inward path. We will examine the biblical call to self-reflection, the psychological insights into the inner workings of our souls, and the spiritual practices that can help us cultivate a deeper relationship with God.

Reflection Questions

1. How has the practice of self-reflection and introspection impacted your personal growth and self-awareness? What tools or techniques have been most helpful for you in this process?

_____

_____

_____

2. Reflect on a time when you resisted or avoided going inward, out of fear, busyness, or distraction. What were the consequences of that avoidance? What did you miss out on by not tending to your inner life?

_____

_____

_____

_____

3. What do you sense God is inviting you to pay attention to in your inner world right now? What parts of yourself are longing for more understanding, compassion, or healing?

_____

_____

_____

Mirror Moment: Imagine you are gazing into a mirror that reflects your soul. What do you see? Journal about the state of your inner life – the thoughts, emotions, longings, and wounds that make up your inner landscape.

Transformative Insights: Reflect on a profound moment of self-discovery or inner transformation that emerged from your own journey of introspection and self-exploration.

1. What new insights, questions, or possibilities arose from this experience, and how have they continued to shape your path and purpose?

_____

_____

_____

2. Consider the transformative power of embracing the journey within, and the ongoing rewards of living a self-examined life.

_____

_____

_____

Perception in Action: Set aside intentional time this week for self-reflection and soul care. Choose a practice that allows you to connect with your inner world, such as journaling, art-making, or contemplative prayer. Notice what emerges as you create space to listen to your life.

Clarity Corner: Reflect on a season of your life when you felt disconnected or out of touch with your inner self. What factors contributed to that sense of disconnection? What practices or choices helped you reconnect with your inner life?

_____

_____

_____

Inner Dialogue Exercise: Imagine a conversation between different parts of yourself (e.g. your inner critic and your inner nurturer, your younger self and your current self). Give voice to their perspectives and needs, and facilitate a dialogue of understanding and integration.

Visionary Prayer: *Intimate God, I open the depths of my being to Your tender presence and loving gaze. Give me the courage to embrace the adventure of self-discovery and the grace to navigate the terrain of my inner world. Illuminate my depths with Your loving presence, and lead me in paths of deepening wholeness and authenticity. In Jesus' name, Amen.*

CHAPTER 20

OVERCOMING IMPOSTOR SYNDROME

Impostor syndrome is the feeling of being a fraud, of not being good enough despite our accomplishments and abilities. For many of us, impostor syndrome is a constant companion, whispering lies of inadequacy and unworthiness that can hold us back from stepping fully into our God-given potential and purpose. In this chapter, we will discover strategies for overcoming limiting beliefs and behaviors. We will examine the truth of our identity and worth, the psychological insights into the nature of self-doubt and self-sabotage, and the practical steps we can take to cultivate greater confidence, courage, and resilience.

Reflection Questions

1. In what areas of your life do you struggle most with feelings of inadequacy, self-doubt, or fraudulence? How do those insecurities impact your confidence and behavior?

_____

_____

_____

2. Reflect on the origins of your impostor syndrome. What messages or experiences from your past have contributed to these feelings of not being "enough"? How can you begin to reframe those narratives through the lens of God's truth?

_____

_____

_____

3. Who are the people in your life who see your gifts, cheer you on, and remind you of your inherent worth? How can you lean into their support and validation when impostor syndrome rears its head?

_____

_____

_____

Mirror Moment: Write a letter to your impostor self, the part of you that doubts your abilities and feels like a fraud. Acknowledge that inner voice with compassion, while also speaking truth and affirmation to counter its lies.

📖 **Transformative Insights:** Reflect on a moment when you challenged or reframed the negative self-talk and limiting beliefs associated with impostor syndrome.

1. What new perspectives or self-affirming truths emerged from this process, and how have they impacted your sense of confidence and capability?

_____

_____

_____

2. Consider the transformative potential of embracing your unique strengths, talents, and achievements, and leading with self-assurance and authenticity.

_____

_____

_____

🚶 **Perception in Action:** Next time you receive a compliment or positive feedback, practice receiving it graciously and internalize it as truth. Resist the urge to deflect or minimize the affirmation, and let it sink into your soul.

💡 **Clarity Corner:** Reflect on a biblical figure who struggled with feelings of inadequacy or impostor syndrome (e.g. Moses, Gideon, Jeremiah). What can you learn from their story about God's faithfulness and sufficiency in the face of self-doubt?

_____

_____

_____

_____

🍴 **Accomplishment Inventory:** Make a list of your accomplishments, skills, and strengths, big and small. Keep it somewhere visible as a reminder of your competence and capability when impostor syndrome strikes.

⛲ **Visionary Prayer:** *Gracious God, I renounce the lies of impostor syndrome and declare the truth of my identity and calling in You. Break off every limitation and insecurity and anoint me with boldness to step into the fullness of my Kingdom destiny. May I live from the unshakable confidence of knowing that You are working powerfully in and through me for Your glory. In Jesus' name, Amen.*

Digital technologies have transformed the way we connect, communicate, and consume information, blurring the lines between the real and the virtual, the public and the private, the true and the false. In this chapter, we will explore the impact of digital technologies and discover the wisdom and discernment needed to thrive in the digital age. We will examine principles for engaging with technology in a way that honors God and others, the psychological insights into the effects of digital media on our mental and emotional well-being, and the practical strategies for cultivating a healthy and balanced relationship with technology.

Reflection Questions

1. How has social media and digital technology impacted your perception of yourself, others, and the world around you – both positively and negatively? What patterns or habits have you noticed in your own engagement with these platforms?

_____

_____

_____

2. Reflect on a time when you compared yourself to someone else's online persona and felt inadequate or discontent. What did that experience reveal about your own insecurities or desires? How can you reframe your perspective in light of God's truth?

_____

_____

_____

3. In what ways have you seen social media used as a tool for connection, creativity, and positive impact? How can you steward your own online presence to reflect your values and make a difference in the digital space?

_____

_____

_____

Mirror Moment: Scroll through your own social media feeds and observe how you curate your online persona. What parts of your life do you highlight or filter out? What messages are you sending about your identity and values?

Transformative Insights: Identify a key insight or lesson you have learned about navigating the challenges and opportunities of the digital age with wisdom, discernment, and intentionality.

1. How has this understanding transformed your relationship with technology and your approach to online communication and connection?

_____

_____

_____

2. Reflect on the importance of cultivating a healthy and balanced digital presence that aligns with your values and supports your personal and spiritual growth.

_____

_____

_____

Perception in Action: Take a social media sabbath for a day or a week, intentionally unplugging from digital platforms to create space for rest, reflection, and real-life connection. Notice how this practice impacts your mental and emotional well-being.

Clarity Corner: Reflect on your relationship with digital technology and identify areas where you need to set clearer boundaries or intentions. What small steps can you take to use these tools more mindfully and purposefully?

_____

_____

_____

_____

Digital Discernment Exercise: Analyze your social media feeds and consider how they shape your perceptions. What voices or influences do you need to limit or unfollow? What sources of truth, beauty, and wisdom could you add?

Visionary Prayer: *Sovereign God, I declare that You are Lord over every realm of my life, including the digital spaces I engage with. I pray for discernment and wisdom to navigate the complexities of this hyperconnected world. May my presence and influence online reflect Your character and invite others into an authentic relationship with You. Let Your Kingdom come in the digital space. In Jesus' name, Amen.*

CHAPTER 22

FULL CIRCLE, THE FINALE

In this final chapter, we'll celebrate your progress and insights while acknowledging that the journey of growth and transformation is a lifelong one. We'll explore what it looks like to integrate the lessons of this book into your daily life and relationships and continue examining and expanding your perceptions. You'll have the opportunity to craft a personal vision for living with greater clarity, compassion, and purpose.

Reflection Questions ❓

1. In what ways have you seen God work through your story and experiences, even the painful and broken parts, to bring about healing and growth in yourself and others?

_____

_____

_____

2. As you look ahead, what new dreams or callings do you sense God placing on your heart? How can you take steps of faith to pursue them, even in the face of fear or uncertainty?

_____

_____

_____

3. How can you use the insights and tools you've gained to make a positive difference in your spheres of influence – your relationships, your work, your community? What unique gifts and perspectives do you bring to the table?

_____

_____

_____

_____

Mirror Moment: Write a letter of gratitude and commitment to yourself, honoring the work you've done and the progress you've made. Affirm your dedication to ongoing growth and learning, and remind yourself of the truths and tools you want to carry forward.

📖 **Transformative Insights:** As you reflect on your journey through this workbook and the transformative insights you have gained along the way, consider how you can continue to integrate and build upon these learnings in your ongoing journey of growth and self-discovery.

1. What new questions, aspirations, or commitments have emerged for you, and how can you continue to cultivate a life of purpose, passion, and authentic expression?

_____

_____

_____

2. Celebrate the progress you have made and the person you are becoming, while embracing the ongoing nature of personal and spiritual transformation.

_____

_____

_____

🚶 **Perception in Action:** Choose one insight, lesson, or skill from this book that feels especially relevant to your life right now. Identify a concrete way you can put it into practice this week, and share your plan with a trusted friend or accountability partner.

💡 **Clarity Corner:** Reflect on how your perceptions of yourself, others, and God have shifted and expanded through this journey. What old lenses or labels have you released? What new truths or possibilities have you embraced?

_____

_____

_____

_____

🏺 **Life Map Exercise:** Create a visual timeline of your life, noting highs, lows, and significant turning points. Reflect on God's faithfulness and the lessons learned in each season. Celebrate your growth!

🙏 **Visionary Prayer:** *Faithful God, thank You for my transformative journey and the revelations You have unlocked within me. Help me to grow in the insights and truths I have gained, while also remaining open to new revelations. Use my story to catalyze change in the lives of others. Anoint me for the new chapter You are writing and lead me forward in the joyful adventure of knowing and reflecting You. In Jesus' name, Amen.*

CONCLUSION

I honor you for the courage, vulnerability, and commitment you have shown in engaging with this material. Examining our lenses, challenging our assumptions, and embracing new perspectives is not easy. It requires a willingness to step outside of our comfort zones, confront uncomfortable truths, and let go of long-held beliefs and behaviors that may no longer serve us. By showing up for this journey, you have demonstrated a desire for growth, healing, and wholeness.

As you move forward from these pages, I encourage you to hold fast to the truths and tools you have gained while also remaining open to ongoing revelation and transformation. Remember that growth is not a destination but a lifelong process marked by both challenges and breakthroughs. There will be moments when you feel stuck, confused, or discouraged, and there will be moments when you experience profound joy, connection, and clarity. Through it all, trust that God is with you, guiding you and shaping you into the fullness of who you were created to be.

I also encourage you to continue seeking out resources, relationships, and experiences that stretch and support you on your journey. Surround yourself with people who challenge you to grow, speak truth and grace into your life, and cheer you on as you step into your God-given purpose.

Above all, remember that you are loved, valued, and purposed by a God who sees you fully and delights in you completely. Your worth is not measured by your productivity, your accomplishments, or your adherence to others' expectations. You are enough, just as you are, and your unique blend of gifts, experiences, and perspectives is needed in this world.

May you continue to seek truth, extend grace, and embrace the beautiful, messy, sacred work of becoming who you were created to be. And may you find joy, purpose, and freedom in the ongoing adventure of living life through the lens of God's love.

> *"Do not conform to the pattern of this world, but be transformed by the renewing of your mind. Then you will be able to test and approve what God's will is—his good, pleasing and perfect will." (Romans 12:2 NIV)*

With gratitude, hope, and expectation for all that lies ahead,
Dr. Taia Willis

NOTES:

_____

_____

_____

_____

_____

_____

_____

_____

_____

_____

_____

_____

_____

_____

_____

_____

_____

_____

_____

_____

_____

_____

www.ingramcontent.com/pod-product-compliance
Lightning Source LLC
LaVergne TN
LVHW080249090426
835508LV00042BA/1497

9 781562 296452